MYSTERIOUS NATURE

VOLCANIC LIGHTNING

BY LISA OWINGS

BELLWETHER MEDIA • MINNEAPOLIS, MN

Torque brims with excitement perfect for thrill-seekers of all kinds. Discover daring survival skills, explore uncharted worlds, and marvel at mighty engines and extreme sports. In *Torque* books, anything can happen. Are you ready?

This edition first published in 2025 by Bellwether Media, Inc.

No part of this publication may be reproduced in whole or in part without written permission of the publisher. For information regarding permission, write to Bellwether Media, Inc., Attention: Permissions Department, 6012 Blue Circle Drive, Minnetonka, MN 55343.

Library of Congress Cataloging-in-Publication Data

LC record for Volcanic Lightning available at: https://lccn.loc.gov/2024009429

Text copyright © 2025 by Bellwether Media, Inc. TORQUE and associated logos are trademarks and/or registered trademarks of Bellwether Media, Inc. Bellwether Media is a division of Chrysalis Education Group.

Editor: Rebecca Sabelko   Designer: Josh Brink

Printed in the United States of America, North Mankato, MN.

TABLE OF CONTENTS

ASH AND LIGHTNING............. 4

WHAT IS
VOLCANIC LIGHTNING? 6

FIERY GODS AND
BRAVE SCIENTISTS 10

IT'S ELECTRIC!..................... 14

GLOSSARY 22

TO LEARN MORE 23

INDEX................................ 24

Ash and Lightning

A volcano **erupts**! Everyone has **evacuated** the area. Crowds watch from a safe distance. **Lava** shoots out of the volcano. A great cloud of ash rises into the air. The sky goes dark.

Suddenly, lightning flashes through the ash cloud. People shout in surprise. Volcanic lightning is a thrilling sight!

What Is Volcanic Lightning?

Volcanoes can erupt in different ways. Some have gentle lava flows with little ash. Others explode. They create huge ash clouds.

lava flow

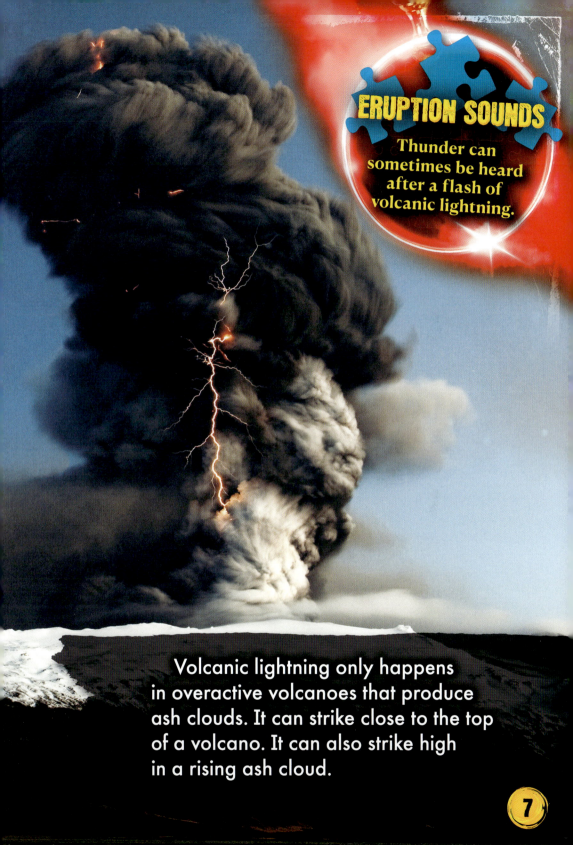

ERUPTION SOUNDS

Thunder can sometimes be heard after a flash of volcanic lightning.

Volcanic lightning only happens in overactive volcanoes that produce ash clouds. It can strike close to the top of a volcano. It can also strike high in a rising ash cloud.

Volcanic lightning is a rare sight. It is most likely to happen at the beginning of large eruptions that create a lot of ash.

Sprites

Sprites are a form of lightning that occur in clouds above thunderstorms. They are often red or orange and last less than a second. Sprites are hard to see from the ground. They often look small, but they can be more than 30 miles (48 kilometers) wide!

Volcanic lightning is most often seen at night. Dark ash clouds can make lightning difficult to see. It is also difficult to see during the day when skies are brighter.

Fiery Gods and Brave Scientists

Volcanic activity has occurred on Earth for billions of years. **Ancient** Romans believed eruptions were the work of Vulcan. This god of fire was a **blacksmith**. He could make lava flow from his **forge**.

Pliny the Younger was the first to write about volcanic lightning. He described it after seeing the deadly blast of Mount Vesuvius in 79 CE.

Pliny the Younger

Blacksmith of the Gods

Ancient Greeks also had a god of fire, Hephaestus. He was also a blacksmith. Some stories state that he helped make Zeus's powerful lightning bolts.

Hephaestus

Scientists studied volcanic lighting for the first time on Mount Vesuvius in the 1800s. It was a dangerous time to study volcanoes. Scientists did not have good tools for the job. Some risked death.

Mount Vesuvius

Hunga Tonga–Hunga Ha'apai Eruption

 Where? southern Pacific Ocean

 When? January 15, 2022

 What happened? The eruption created an ash cloud that rose at least 36 miles (58 kilometers) into the air. Its lightning storm lasted 11 hours. Lightning flashed up to 2,600 times per minute!

Satellites and other tools have made the work safer. Scientists study the lightning from a distance. But it can still be hard to **predict** or see.

It's Electric!

Lightning is the result of **static electricity**. Most objects are electrically **neutral**. When objects rub together, **electrons** can jump from one object to another. This changes the charge of both objects.

static electricity

The object with more electrons becomes negatively charged. The other becomes positively charged. This charge difference is static electricity.

Volcanic lightning happens when static electricity builds up in an ash cloud. Some parts of the cloud take on a negative charge. Others have a positive charge.

ash cloud

Scientists think static electricity builds up when ash **particles** rub together. They also believe it can happen when water that is high up in the cloud freezes. Ice crystals rub together. This creates a charge difference.

LIGHTNING MINUS THE VOLCANO

Ice also causes lightning in regular storms. Small ice crystals rub against larger ones high in the clouds. This creates static electricity and lightning.

Charge differences in ash clouds set the stage for volcanic lightning. Negative and positive charges **attract** each other. They want to be in balance. The extra electrons in a negatively charged ash cloud seek a path to neutral.

How Volcanic Lightning Forms

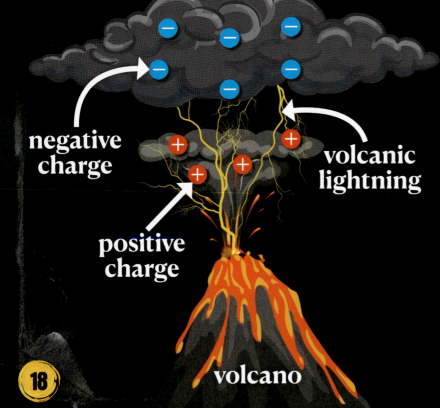

negative charge

positive charge

volcanic lightning

volcano

A bolt of lightning forms when a path is found. It jumps to the nearest area of positive charge. The lightning **restores** the balance.

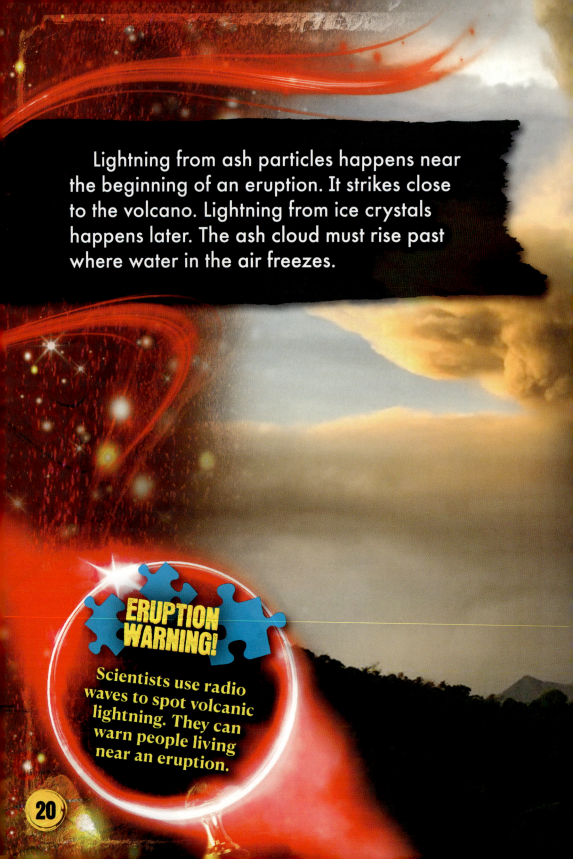

Lightning from ash particles happens near the beginning of an eruption. It strikes close to the volcano. Lightning from ice crystals happens later. The ash cloud must rise past where water in the air freezes.

ERUPTION WARNING!

Scientists use radio waves to spot volcanic lightning. They can warn people living near an eruption.

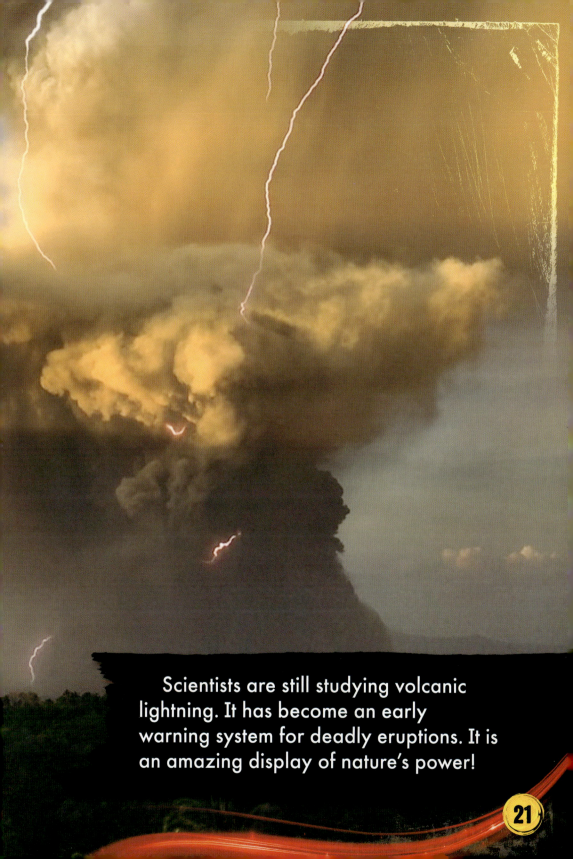

Scientists are still studying volcanic lightning. It has become an early warning system for deadly eruptions. It is an amazing display of nature's power!

GLOSSARY

ancient—from long ago

attract—to cause something to move closer

blacksmith—a person who heats and shapes metal to create tools and other objects

electrons—tiny particles with a negative electric charge

erupts—forces out lava and ash

evacuated—moved away from a dangerous area

forge—a furnace or workshop where blacksmiths heat and shape metal

lava—hot, liquid rock that flows from a volcano

neutral—not electrically charged

particles—tiny bits of matter; matter is materials that form objects and take up space.

predict—to guess what will happen in the future

restores—returns something to its original condition

satellites—human-made objects that circle Earth; satellites are used for communication and collecting data.

static electricity—an imbalance in electric charges often caused by objects rubbing together

TO LEARN MORE

AT THE LIBRARY

Mikoley, Kate. *Thunder and Lightning.* Buffalo, N.Y.: Gareth Stevens Publishing, 2024.

Oachs, Emily Rose. *Pompeii.* Minneapolis, Minn.: Bellwether Media, 2020.

Romero, Libby. *All About Volcanoes.* New York, N.Y.: Children's Press, 2021.

ON THE WEB

FACTSURFER

Factsurfer.com gives you a safe, fun way to find more information.

1. Go to www.factsurfer.com

2. Enter "volcanic lightning" into the search box and click 🔍.

3. Select your book cover to see a list of related content.

INDEX

ash, 5, 6, 8, 17, 20
ash cloud, 5, 6, 7, 9, 16, 17, 18, 20
blacksmith, 10, 11
electrons, 14, 15, 18
erupts, 5, 6, 8, 10, 13, 20, 21
explanation, 14, 15, 16, 17, 18, 19, 20
Hephaestus, 11
history, 10, 11, 12, 13
how volcanic lightning forms, 18
Hunga Tonga-Hunga Ha`apai Eruption, 13
ice crystals, 17, 20
lava, 5, 6, 10

Mount Vesuvius, 10, 12
Pliny the Younger, 10
radio waves, 20
satellites, 13
sprites, 9
static electricity, 14, 15, 16, 17
thunder, 7
tools, 12, 13
volcano, 5, 6, 7, 12, 20
Vulcan, 10
warning, 20, 21
water, 17, 20

The images in this book are reproduced through the courtesy of: Christian Hartmann, front cover (hero); plampy, front cover (lightning); Marc Szeglat/picture-alliance/dpa/AP Images/ AP Newsroom, pp. 2-3, 22-24; Anadolu/ Getty Images, pp. 4-5; Ralf Lehmann, p. 6 (lava flow); Erlend Haarberg/naturepl.com/ Alamy, pp. 6-7; Kerstin Langenberger/ Alamy, pp. 8-9; Asa Schlobohm, p. 9; Geoffrey/ Wiki Commons, p. 10 (Pliny the Younger); PhotoFires, pp. 10-11; SuperStock/Piemags/PL Photography Limited, p. 11 (Hephaestus); Belish, pp. 12-13; NOAA/ Alamy, p. 13; vitaldrum, p. 14 (static electricity); Kyodo/ AP Newsroom, pp. 14-15; Mario Dalma Leon, pp. 16-17; Anatolia, p. 18 (How Volcanic Lightning Forms); Mike Lyvers/ Getty Images, pp. 18-19; Michael Anthony Sagaran, pp. 20-21; fboudrias, back cover.